TERSELY YOURS

VOLUME III

Haiku Poetry in Defense of Nature For The Coming Spiritual-Ecological Age

BY

VIC HUMMERT

TERSELY YOURS

~ Volume III ~

First Printing 1998

Published by

Earth Literacy Press
122 Rosedale
Lafayette, LA 70508

Library of Congress Catalog Number: 97-95035
ISNB 0-9667189-1-7

Book Production by Portier Gorman, Inc. 1-888-273-2352
Printed in the USA by Morris Publishing • Kearney, NE 68847

In memory of my brother,
Captain Thomas Hummert,
who died at age 28
in a B-17 bomber,
May 5th, 1945

"War is not women's' history."

-Virginia Wolf

"The greatest thing
a human being ever does in this world
is to see something.
To see something is poetry,
prophecy and religion all in one."

-John Ruskin, 1819-1900,
English writer and social critic

Acknowledgments

"Many things in life seem expensive, but we get a free trip around the Sun each year." (*The Catholic Digest*, June 1998.)

My first acknowledgment, however humble, is to God for the gift of time. Those of you who read ***Tersely Yours Volume I*** know that it was a brain tumor which prompted me to write a three-line, 17-syllable verse - a haiku:

We cannot outrun a brain tumor
So just relax
And call it "friend"

That verse was written in 1993, twenty years after the first brain surgery in 1973. My fascination with Japanese poetry and the brevity of Cantonese-Chinese brought me to the point of always carrying a small notebook for writing haiku poems.

I am grateful to Maryknoll for thirty years in a Society which reaches out to people who are considered "God's anawhim" (the little and forgotten ones).

I am thankful for having had the opportunity to make many visits to people under hospice care in the Lafayette area. After opting to resign from the priesthood I was able to experience the angst of over 100,000 GM workers who will eventually lose their jobs because CEO's will follow the television industry to other countries where millions are unemployed and will work for $1 a day.

With that emptiness of being unemployed I was able to feel more gratitude for the gift of time while searching for a steady job.

My gratitude to so many of you who encouraged me to keep on with the writing. My thanks to Jacques who likes to hear a haiku or two over the phone while he is at work.

My gratitude to Bob Chaney who tried in vain to help me use a computer. Every computer in the world feels my anger at a technology which sacrifices thousands of young workers. Their eyes go bad after a few years squinting at those tiny chips.

Roselyn, my patient wife, has been very tolerant as I respond to the encouragement of people who want to see more poems. These gifts of time and encouragement allowed me to rewrite Volume I, then complete II and III during the time of "having no work."

Vic Hummert
June 29, 1998
Feast of SS Peter and Paul,
who founded the church
after resolving discord
over non-Jewish membership.

INTRODUCTION

This book is a love story of one man's love affair with the Earth. In every word that he writes one feels his passion for his lover. His pain moves us when we feel his suffering for his lover in agony, suffering from abuse and neglect. His only desire is to make his lover happy. Although he is unable to heal her pain, he stays by her side offering consolation. His consolation is in the form of haiku Poetry. Each Haiku expresses his desire to heal her brokenness. Unknowingly, the author has become a modern day prophet. He is calling each of us to become aware of the great harm we are causing his lover. He is pleading with us to turn away from our callous actions toward the Earth.

Like all prophets, the author has an important message for each of us. He forsees the coming catastrophe. He sees that the catastrophe is already upon us. It has touched our lives at Love Canal, in the East River in New York City, in the Delta of Mississippi, and in the bodies of soldiers sent to observe nuclear blasts in the Nevada desert. It touches our lives from a distance. The smoke from fires in Mexico pollutes the skies of North America. The shrimp farmers in Vietnam pollute the seas to serve the appetites of hungry people in first world countries. There is no place to run. There is no longer any place to hide. The Earth resists this abuse. We are victims and perpetrators. The economic lust of Wall Street guides our every move. This lust for money has transformed us into a consumer society. As we consume more, we demand more. Our appetites are insatiable. Our culture is consumed with material consumption. There are few voices among our leaders. There are few voices that challenge us to new ways of living. There are only voices calling out of the darkness warning us of our impending doom. The sounds of these voices are soft and often silent. Yet, they are not silent. We are deaf. The voices are loud and constant. However, they are not heard over the clanging and screaming of the masses who are controlled by those whose only responsibility is to stockholders.

Is there no hope? Is our destiny determined? Are we, as a people, destined to destroy the Earth and life on the Earth? For the children of the Creator there is always hope. Our God sends men and women in every generation to give us hope. Our hope lies in listening to the prophets that are sent to us in every age. In our generation hearts of hope surround us. There is a heart beating in our midst. Vic Hummert, the author of this book, is one the prophets. He is a prophet of love. Vic is a man of great compassion for people of the Earth. Vic's book, ***Tersely Yours, Volume III,*** is a call for humanity to reconcile with the Earth. How well we listen to Vic's voice may determine our future.

Vic has taught me many lessons. He taught me to be a voice for the voiceless. He taught me that life is more fully lived when it is lived simply. He taught me that the best witness is often the silent, visible witness. It is a witness who communicates through their life. Vic's life speaks volumes. It is a life of deep humility and sincere simplicity. It would bring joy to Vic's heart if he knew that his words transformed the attitude of his brothers and sisters on this planet toward the Earth. His quest is a hero's quest. This hero's quest is to create solidarity between the Earth and its human inhabitants. As John Paul 11 said, "Solidarity seeks to go beyond itself, to take on the specifically Christian dimensions of total gratitude, forgiveness, and reconciliation." It is time to forge the bonds of solidarity with our planet and to heed the words of her prophets.

Raymond L. Calabrese, Professor
The University of Texas at San Antonio
San Antonio, Texas, June 11, 1998

PREFACE

Where can I find a man[1] who has forgotten words?
He is the one I would like to talk to.
- Chuang Tzu
(4th century B.C.)

Of what value is a man who has forgotten words? If historian Lewis Mumford is correct, there would be no such thing as a 'man,' were it not for words. "Man's (sic) greatest need in emerging from animalhood was to transform himself; and the chief instruments of his awakening consciousness were his own gestures and sounds reflected and imitated in those of his fellow creatures." Mumford suggests that only by the language that words enable were the first 'human' minds capable of connecting, interacting, and learning. By words our ancestors were empowered to teach children, write histories, and create cultures and civilizations. Surely words have allowed us to transform ourselves into better creatures. What, then, could we possibly hope to learn from a man who has forgotten words?

C.S. Lewis once observed that "the better stuff a creature is made of - the cleverer and stronger and freer it is - then the better it will be if it goes right, but also the worse it will be if it goes wrong." Because words transformed us by making us cleverer, stronger, and freer creatures, we would do well to examine them, particularly in cases where we do not seem to be getting any better. In our relationship with the Earth, for example, we have been getting worse for several thousand years, with the past few centuries witnessing unprecedented extremes of ecologically disastrous human behavior. Might our destructive conduct have something to do with our words? Environmental philosopher Niel Evernden answers in the affirmative, arguing that the environmental movement has accomplished little and will continue to fail until it critically examines the role that language has played in engendering our current dilemma.

There is no shortage of books documenting the scientific and technological revolutions which have brought us to the precipice of disaster. But the "band-aids" of better technology which these books would have us apply to the symptoms of planetary pathology will do little to heal its deeper origin. More thoughtful scholars have noted that the scientific and rational thinking which afforded technological control over nature would not have been allowed to take control had it not also fostered a worldview in which nature was reduced to a mere object, empty of meaning, purpose, and value.

In his book, ***The Social Creation of Nature***, Niel Evernden argues that changes in the Western worldview were mediated by changes in language. These changes did not escape the notice of Lewis Mumford, who writes, "... from the beginning [language] was an instrument for embracing the living body of human experience, not just the bleached articulated skeleton of definable ideas." The transformations of language observed by Mumford and Evernden took place at the same time scientific thinking gained ascendancy in Western culture, for reason and rational argument demanded that words be stripped of their ambiguities and symbolic meanings. In Evernden's terminology, words necessarily became "conceptual containers" in order to afford "a grasp on something which defies easy containment, something large and intractable" (the natural world, for example). In Evernden's analysis, our language/worldview/environmental problems actually began during the first age of reason with the invention of the word "Nature." He writes, "all of creation became our object when the Greeks were able to capture it in a word-cage."

If Evernden is correct, advocates for a more responsible relationship to the natural world have been unknowingly disarmed before the battle begins. We have little choice but to enter the debate in the accepted language of our culture. Unfortunately, word-cages constructed for the purpose of dispassionate, rational discourse are inherently incapable of conveying the profound meaning of our cause. To make matters worse, the modern rise of reason, which began with the Renaissance, has turned the other edge of its blade against the meaning, purpose, and value of the natural world. Quentin Smith writes, "the assumption that reasoning can be the only means of discovering a meaning of the world has been the guiding idea of philosophical investigations since the time of Plato. But for over a century now... reason has been demonstrated to be incapable of comprehending such a meaning, and thus, if the only meaning the world is capable of possessing is a rationally discernible meaning, the conclusion becomes unavoidable that the world is meaningless."

No wonder, then, that the modern environmental movement has accomplished so little. We arm ourselves with words which will allow us to present reasonable arguments, without understanding that the passion which compels those arguments is twice reduced in conforming to cultural standards of 'reasonable'. Where can I find a man who has forgotten words?

It would seem that we need to look to the East, where reason has not completely displaced all other ways of apprehending the meaning of the world. Zen Buddhism, for example, possesses a most profound understanding of the problem of words. "The practitioner of the Way must enter into direct contact with reality without allowing concepts to separate him/her from this reality. Reality cannot be conceived, nor can it be described in words," writes Thich Nhat Hanh. If we could only persuade all parties involved in a given environmental debate to meditate to the point of 'awakening' prior to deliberation, we might achieve better outcomes. Unfortunately, this possibility is sufficiently remote to demand that we look elsewhere.

"What we need is a new conversation," suggests Neil Evernden, "one in which the voices permitted are not limited to those of practical activity and science." His sentiment is echoed by Richard Rorty, who writes, "a talent for speaking differently, rather than for arguing well, is the chief instrument of cultural change." Where can I find a man who has forgotten that words have become cages? It is apparently he that we need to talk to.

"Every word was once a poem," writes Emerson. "The etymologist finds the deadest word to have been once a brilliant picture. Language is fossil poetry." Emerson believed that the poet was singularly gifted with the ability to craft living language capable of shattering its cages and expressing the transcendent meaning of the world. "Every thought is also a prison... Therefore we love the poet. He unlocks our chains, and admits us to a new scene." Where can I possibly find a poet who has forgotten words? Might there be such a thing as Zen poetry?

The "wordless poem," according to Alan Watts, one of Zen Buddhism's greatest Western advocates, is the haiku. In his little book entitled ***The Wordless Poem***, Eric Amman writes, "the technique of wordlessness... as we find it in both Zen and haiku, is to avoid [the] confusion between words and realities." Amman quotes the haiku poet R. H. Blythe, who maintains that "a haiku is not literature inasmuch as it dispenses with words as much as possible." Haiku, then, is a deliberate attempt to transcend the constrictions of conceptual containers; by "wordlessness" haiku reclaims the ability of language to embrace the living body of our experience, an experience radiant with meaning and purpose.

Where can I find a wordless poet? I have found him in the pages which follow, as will you. For there are no word-cages in the haiku of Vic Hummert. Rather, he has crafted word-gems so finely cut and polished that they radiate, rather than imprison, the sacred meaning of all that lives. Nor are there arguments here; Vic has made no attempt to persuade by reason. He has merely provided unmediated revelations of existential reality, revelations which shatter our word-bound concepts and awaken the passion which compels justice, peace, and responsibility in our relationship with the living Earth. I can illustrate Vic's gift in no better way than to allow him to wordlessly illuminate that which I have wasted several pages of trees (largely spent arguing a path through an obfuscating word-forest of my own construction) attempting to convey.

When reasoning is dormant
Vic's[2] haiku breaks through sleep
To touch our hearts

- E. Griff Blakewood, Ph.D.
Lafayette Louisiana
June, 1998

1-In this, and several other quotations there exists an antiquated gender bias. Rather than encumber the text with numerous [sic] notations, I have allowed this bias to remain. Because the preface is ultimately about a 'man' (i.e. Vic Hummert), I hope that my decision will be understood, or at least forgiven.

2-"You're short a syllable," Vic mentioned, when first sharing this haiku with me, suggesting that I add the word 'Good' at the beginning of the second line. I believe my alternative of using the author's name to be the better solution.

God and money
Are never asleep
One gives Life, the other drains us

We are "Stardust"
Made of longing
For the Source of all Light[1]

When our license states:
"Do not eat this fish often"
Recall some folks can't read

We cannot live by
Faith alone
Wisdom calls us to be practical

Life without songs
Of whippoorwills
Is spiritual deprivation

1-Everything in our cosmos emanates from the original Big Birth of a star some fifteen billion years ago. Scientists estimate planet Earth is approximately five billion years old.

Wander from Truth[1]
Then we lose sight of
God's loving face, peaceful presence

In our high-tech age
Of global communications
Who speaks with Earth?

We are - each one
Bright shooting stars
Meteorites in conscious action

Our true self before
God is being lovable and
Loving children

1-As stated in ***Tersely Yours, Volume II,*** for Gandhi, God is Truth.

"Walk into death
With our eyes wide open"
Free acceptance of new life[1]

Place more trust in women
Switch to eating more rice[2]
For great cosmic changes

Enough of empty words
We have known for years
What must be changed

Whither the churches
In our next century
Depends upon health of Earth

1-Latin American wisdom (Entramus en la muerte con los ojos abiertos) is in sync with the late Saul Alinsky, a fearless community organizer who declared: "Once we have accepted our death, we are free to live for the first time."

2-Albert Einstein advocated a gradual transition to a vegetarian diet for improvement in one's health and alleviation of the biological pressure upon Earth from billions of animals which compete for food with billions of human beings. The population is estimated to be 6.2 billion people in the late 1990's. In the United States, 50% of the land is used for livestock, pasture and range. Over half of the grain produced in the United States goes to feeding animals.

Disregarding rank
Sunrise and Tokyo subways
Wait for nobody

When friends fear
Loss of kin
Strive to be ersatz family to them

Life is the following out
Of our birth hour's mandate
To leave comfort

Amid bloody struggles over land
Earth states: "I'm not yours;
Soon you are mine"

Have no ambition besides
Compassion and care
For those around us[1]

1-Anthropologist Ashley Montague defines a civilized society as a "considerate society."

As Earth personified[1]
Why must we wage wars
Against our own bodies?

Our profit system
Now legalizes rape
Of children, women, men

Fiber optics
Cannot relate one simple message
From Earth to us

If we follow laws
To the extreme
Compassion will be suffocated

1- The Jesuit priest, mystic and scientist, Teilhard de Chardin, integrated science and spirituality in teaching us that we are Earth taking on flesh and consciousness. Chardin was born in 1881 and died in 1955. His numerous writings help us perceive how humankind is evolving into a spiritual plateau. Teilhard's writings strive to bring us to a fuller realization that we are the Earth loving, reflecting, hoping for the future of life on the planet.

As first and last of a kind
Each encounter of life
Calls for our best

Our loving God
Is no farther from each one
Than our very next breath

Our lives like candles
Can give light, warmth
Inspiration till the end

Boundless compassion
Our eternal flame
Whose light will never die out

In one moment
God's Sun gives more energy
Than in our whole story

Cars are as
Spreading termites
In the cosmic cocoon which gives us life[1]

Selfless love includes
Pursuit of those goals
Which lie beyond our vision

Our sunset in life
Earth opens loving arms
To gently receive us

With access to
World wide webs and endless widgets
Are we any wiser?

1-As stated in ***Tersely Yours, Volume II*** (p. 62), there were only one million cars when Thomas Berry was born in 1914. In the 21st century there will be over 600 million. China has joined the rush to urban gridlock with over 100 car companies now operating in the new economic structure.

One glass of water
Just a cent (.01¢)
Bottled water - seven hundred cents[1]

"Can we drink the water here?"
Now a question
In rich and poor nations

If rejected by
Blind academes[2]
Know that Earth cherishes us still

When we ignore warnings
Lessons are learned later
In harsh, drastic ways[3]

1-The cost of a drink of bottled water is estimated to be 700 times more than a glass of water from the tap. Since potable drinking water is a luxury in many parts of Latin America, the people drink four-to-five times more soda than water because bottling companies treat the water first. Obviously, this is an expense.

2-The noted child psychologist, Erik Eriksen, even though teaching at Harvard, did not have a college degree. At the time of his death in 1993. *The New York Times* gave nearly a full page to his obituary.

3-Geologists confirm the number of earthquakes has risen continually with the onset of atomic detonations throughout the world. The most recent was a quake in Afghanistan following five nuclear blasts by India, then Pakistan's response with five more atomic detonations in the Spring of 1998.

Despite our disruptions
Earth has remained
Faithful for billions of years

Gas once sold cheap as water
Now water is
Costly as gasoline[1]

Our Sun always faithful
Calling us to follow
That same Divine Voice

Each heartbeat our gift
Every breath a miracle
Given without cost

Since all we have are gifts
We are wise to
Excel in humility

1-A gallon of water in supermarkets could be the same price, or more, than a gallon of gasoline.

In Jesus we see
Who God truly is
Who we are called to become

Pollution knows no boundaries
Calls for new
Meaning of security[1]

One trillion spent
On arms each year[2]
Leaves us all insecure

Conscience alone will stop
Our wasting one million
Per minute on arms

1-In 1998, traces of radioactivity are still found in the Alps from the 1987 Chernobyl nuclear accident.

2-Can a global economy which spends over $1 trillion yearly on arms survive indefinitely? In the *World Military & Social Expenditures*, Ruth Leger Sivard and staff researchers estimate nations of the world are squandering far more on training soldiers than educating children.

Rising sea levels
On island nations
One silent form of warfare

The boy wore a bracelet[1]
With a simple question
What Would Jesus Do?

Truly - where is God
Calling each one through Earth
To be creatures of Love?

If every breath is a prayer[2]
Drawn in gratitude
What need for words?

1-A red cloth bracelet with gold letters: W.W.J.D.

2-Hasidic Jews look upon each breath as a prayer in union with the "Rhuah" (Spirit or breath of One who is beyond the descriptive power of words).

In our moments of weakness
Not perfection
God's Spirit draws closer

Everything in our whole cosmos
Flows from One
Divine Spirit of Love

To inhale with thanks
And exhale with trust
Makes us one with the Spirit

We falsely presume
There is endless room
For more planes, cars, mounds of trash

When fetid garbage is dumped
Why does it not fall
Near the affluent?

Even when killing ourselves[1]
We all strongly resent
Changing our ways

When the beloved is ready
A faithful lover
Will soon appear

Like small leaves
In big typhoons[2]
We are swept along by surprise events

1-Bishop Michael Pfeiffer of San Angelo, Texas joined spiritual leaders in Guatemala and the Philippines who witness a steady decline in the quality of air, water and vanishing topsoil which produces our food. He raised a question which is now quite possible, indeed, a reality in certain regions of the world: "Y que si la tierra no fuese habitable?"
("And what if the land becomes uninhabitable?"
- *El Visitante*, San Antonio, 24th January 1993)

2-"Typhoon" is a corruption of the Cantonese Chinese word "daaih fung," meaning great wind.

Hospice patients are blessed
With the grace to know
This is my life's last year[1]

Ours is one constant effort
In drawing closer
To a loving God

We can define true life
As trying always
To be one with God's words

Unless churches join with God
To preserve Earth
Our children have no future

Each snowflake
Takes on unique form
Only through our Divine Designer

1-From 1995 - 1998 I served as chaplain to the terminally ill in the Lafayette, Louisiana area, making nearly 3000 visits to the sick and dying under the care of Hospice of Acadiana Hospice patients are accepted only if diagnosed as having six months or less to live.

"Birds have nests"[1]
But homeless daughters and sons
Have nowhere to lay their heads

We witness eternity each day
As sunshine kisses
Our seas with love

Songbirds daily manifest
Grace, music
Colors of a loving God

Each breath, every heartbeat
One time endowments
From a Divine Source

If we just see
One answer to our climate change
Rises every morning

1-Matthew 8:20 and Luke 9:58. In the summer of 1998, a friend arrived in Lafayette by rail. Exhausted, he fell asleep on the railroad track. The empty cars nearby were hooked up by a switch engine in the area. Suddenly Chrishtopher awoke in unspeakable pain as the steel wheels cut off his right arm.

Those born before Hiroshima[1]
Are the last
Healthy generation

Mindfulness of our eternal now
Frees us from
Tension and worry

In challenging moments of life
We seek a double portion
Of God's Spirit

When our spirit shakes loose
In that last breath
We savor total freedom

1-This claim is made by Sister Rosalie Bertell, an epidemiologist of international renown and author of ***No Immediate Danger***. Her book documents the impact of radioactivity upon all of us. The documentary film *Antarctica* shows how this pristine region of Earth has traces of radioactivity, petroleum by-products and carbon dioxide in ice cores drilled 600 feet into the ice. That which permeates ice cores has stolen into our bone marrow as well.

Acceptance of looming death
In major surgery
Our act of faith

"Sweetheart, keep life simple"
Proceed - in firm kindness
Cloaked in gratitude

When half our given years
Have passed
We double our thanks for the rest

The next century
One more chance in learning
How to befriend our Earth

Earth strives lovingly
To place us in the locus
We are meant to be

Sunshine smiles warmly on us daily
Even when others
Look askance

We are all reptiles, mammals[1]
Who strive daily
For higher consciousness

God's divine cosmos
Poised in "no - thing - ness"[2]
Yet moves smoother than Swiss watches

Boundless Spirit
Through Nature opening our dim eyes
Might save us still

1-Neuro-scientists tell of three distinct levels in the human brain - the reptilian, mammalian and the point to which we are called to become - creatures of higher consciousness.

2-Job 26:7

We taste salvation
When our Compassion includes
God's entire cosmos

Grief at loss of loved ones
Yearning for union
With One who gives all life

Each one serves
As a loving presence
Not absence of God to others

While rivers worldwide
Strive to survive
Where does healthcare begin for us?

If our air is now lethal
What hope remains
For lungs of all creatures?

Before one word came from his mouth
Jesus was a threat
To big powers[1]

Direct clear daily
Access to God
Lies in our heartbeat and breathing

We all flow from You
And pine for the moment
We will return to Love

You save us by pouring
Justice, Truth
With Compassion into our lives

The longest journey
We shall make
Is to move from our head to the heart

1-To protect himself, Herod ordered the slaying of all male infants in the Bethlehem region (Matthew 2:16).

Earth alone
Has the power[1]
To prevent greed from destroying ourselves

Greed over fossil fuels
Brings on wars which
Delay our solar age[2]

Fools will state
Our bottom line is profit
Wisdom knows it is pure air

1-Catastrophic events of Nature - floods, droughts, quakes and violent windstorms - are manifestations of Earth "fighting back" against corporate plundering when warnings of scientists do not have the capacity to bring about modification of the global profit system.

2-Technology already exists to begin the shift to wind and solar energy in industrialized nations. However, the automobile (Daimler-Benz + Chrysler in 1998) and energy corporations are listed among the top 100 global economic powers. They will not benefit from wind and sun which cannot be metered. And thus, greed driven by blindness carries us into struggles for control of sources of energy. The United States alone imports over 16 million barrels of oil each day.

Leave thoughts which
Regret the past, fear our future
Just give thanks for now-here

Our brief lives are
Rapture in Love
Not torture from tensions

With three deft lines
Seventeen syllables
Haiku sees Nature as God does

In the Genesis creation drama
God would not
Brook loneliness[1]

There is simply no simpler message
We are all called
To save our Earth

1-"It is not good to be alone." (Genesis 2:18)

We can not expect
To be defenders of truth
Without suffering

Ecology will become
Our bedrock
Of all other disciplines

Basho[1] invites all
In times of waiting, boredom
Write good haiku poems

Roses must give up their glory
Return to Earth who
Brings forth more beauty

1-Basho is the adopted name of Matsuo Munefusa (1644-1694), a Japanese poet who became master of the haiku. In the Japanese vowel-consonant, vowel-consonant structure of each word, the haiku poems were lines of 5, 7 and 5 syllables. Basho made the haiku an accepted form of poetic expression in Japan. Haiku poetry written in English need not adhere to the strict syllabic formation. (As explained above.)

In the great fury of winter storms
Nature alone
Retains power[1]

Accept our daily miracles
Just breathing and heartbeats
Then let thanks flow

If discovered
Jet fumes lace our planet with poison
Would we fly less?

We are facing
The most awesome
Spiritual challenge of our story`

1 -"Nature is the only power here now." Comment of a utility repairman following an ice storm in the winter of 1998 which left parts of Canada without electricity for days.

If we forbid
Harmful drugs within
Why permit destructive feelings?

Allow not one negative thought
Between a loving God
And ourselves

Clear mind-ful-ness feels
This loving God in our breathing
Heartbeat, walking

If not concerned
About history[1]
Drowsiness dominates reason

1-Not until the 20th century have we had the real capacity to destroy Earth. Since every institution within which we function today is pre-atomic in nature, they are obsolete. The academic centers which are designed to foster peace, non-violence and care of our threatened environment are relevant. However, these departments are located on universities where the vast majority of students are enrolled in courses which must maintain the status quo.

If we go to the center
Of the eye in our heart[1]
God awaits us

One temple which provides
Peaceful sanctuary for
God is our heart[2]

Show no anger
To one who ignores you
Silence as violence is theirs[3]

Our story will never shatter
Earth's faithful
Journey about the Sun

1-While in Hong Kong I heard this haunting question: "In the center of the eye in your heart, who do you wish to be, or what do you want to do?"

2-One of the quotes written in the ceiling of the Library of Congress states: "There is only one temple - it is the heart of all men." (To which I add - women)

3-In the 1970's, while asking a group of grammar school students to list all the means of violence against others - fists, knives, clubs, guns, bombs, missiles - a 4th grade boy raised his little voice and said: "Silence is violence"

Faithful flaming Sun
Calls us daily
To break fossil fuel addictions

Be peaceful since every fear
Is a mini-fear
Of our fear of death

Fewer words
With deeper silence
Bring our compassionate God closer

Listen for
The soft voice of God
Rather than opinions of others

Tomorrow isn't real
One absolute is God's gift
Of our next breath

Colonies have gone
Leaving corporations
To dominate our world

Each breath is the fullness
Of God's life
Giving us hearts of compassion

Our lungs always
Prefer sacred oxygen
over "development"

I breathe
Therefore I am[1]
Forever united to a loving God

It is God through Nature
Who determines our future
For weal or woe

1-René Descartes (1596-1650) said: "Cogito, ergo sum" (I think, therefore I am.) The comic strip characters FRANK & ERNEST by Bob Thaves add: "I think... therefore I worry"

Placing our bodies
Where the words are[1]
Results in painful suffering

Finding peace
With one's conscience
Is more important than security

Through our loving Earth
We are called to speak
For air, water, soil

We are Earth
Taking on body, soul, loving
Awareness and care of self

We will always speak
In defense of Truth
Because God and Truth are One

1-The Chinese word for faith, trust, belief is a person standing alongside her or his words.

Before churches were hewn from forests
We found the Divine
In Nature[1]

If breast milk is now tainted[2]
Is it not time to
Ask what we are about?

For billions of years
Sun, Moon and stars
Have arrived on time to guide us

May all of our years
Be pleasing to God
True loving gift to others

1-Simple surveys indicate many people find spiritual experiences in Nature, in music, then among loving and supportive friends and family.

2-See *Rachel's Health & Environment Weekly, #193*, August 8th, 1990 to find documentation regarding over 100 industrial chemicals now found in the purest form of human nutrition. Rachel's is an excellent, inexpensive weekly newsletter, one page in length. It provides astounding, well-researched information on the state of our Earth. P.O.Box 5036, Annapolis, MD 21403

Our sacred role to remind all
We can't live as
The last generation

Becoming wealthy is a dream
Of those who are
Bankrupt in spirit

A tyranny of "progress"
Removes our trees
Smothers blessed land with roads

"Going about doing good"[1]
Is our best pathway
To peace and meaning

Words are like keys
Smoothly honed
To open doors of understanding

1-"Jesus went about doing good..." (Acts of the Apostles 10:38)

What happens to rivers
Is just the manner
In which we poison ourselves

Look into the sad eyes[1]
Of wounded owls
Find God seeking mercy through Nature

Children who have not heard
The Nutcracker or whippoorwill
Are deprived

Someone who is not
Going through change at all times
Is in fact - regressing

Someday soon grief counseling
Will extend to
Death of rivers and lakes

1-Two women who work for Animals in Distress in Lafayette (Louisiana) brought a permanently wounded owl to the monthly Sierra Club meeting for a face-to-face encounter.

Rejection is our share
In God's pain[1]
When we refuse fullness of Life

Could not the One
Who brings sunrise on time
Plan our lives to the minute?

We seek a double portion
Of God's Spirit
To lavish upon all

Nudging great icebergs
Could be easier
Than changing human consciousness

People who despise
And resent us
Don't allow our spirit to live

1-The "pain" God feels is akin to loving parents who find their offerings of love and care rebuffed by their own children.

Remember we are
From God through Earth
Who beckons us to return home[1]

In the center of the eye
Of our heart
God alone resides, guides us

When we "Have No Head"[2]
For worry or fear
God's peace reigns in our calm hearts

We live always in God's presence
Our moment for Truth,
Compassion and Love

1-Ash Wednesday liturgical words of the minister who places ashes upon the foreheads of those who attend. "Remember, you are from Earth, and to Earth you shall return."

2-On ***Having No Head*** is a book written by D.E. Harding in 1988. The subject is Zen practice.

We remain in Your gentle hands
While stars smile upon us
Guide our course

Even if someone tried to kill me
I would still be
Moved to forgive[1]

We are in full presence
Of our God who calls us
To more awareness

There is a limit
To the Judas experiences
We can bear

1-While working with the British government official who spoke on behalf of the deprived people in Hong Kong, I recall an angry man who phoned with the threat to kill all of us for our outspoken positions. We who worked in Mrs. Elsie Elliott-Tu's ward office reacted in a tolerant and forgiving manner and did not miss one hour of listening to 100 people each week who came seeking advice for personal problems.

Our salvation is
Living out God's deep compassion
For all beings

Each breath is pure gift
From our loving God
Who desires to give full Life[1]

Our "information age"
Will stimulate deep changes
Or remain mere gossip

Although beyond our strength
We are called daily
To love all as God does

1-John 10:10

"Farewell"[1] if said
With deep faith
Is really a call to draw closer to the Divine

"What if life on Earth
Becomes impossible?"[2]
Now our practical question

A boundless Spirit
Propels our expanding Universe
And conscience

Brave truth from My Lai
Lay buried for thirty years
Then rose in glory[3]

1-Acts of the Apostles 23:30
2-Bishop Michael Pfeiffer, writing in El Visitante, January 24th, 1993 raised the question - "Y que Si la tierra no fuese habitable?" (And what if the land becomes uninhabitable?) (c.f. p. 26, f.n. 1)
3-When Hugh Thompson discovered U.S. troops killing civilians near My Lai, Vietnam, he followed his conscience and gave orders to his own unit to kill the U.S. soldiers, lead by Lt. Robert Calley. Thompson was given a special award in the Easter season of 1998. Later, he was given a peace citation conferred upon Gandhi & Mother Teresa. Lt. Calley, although found guilty of war crimes, has not served one day in jail and operates a jewelry business in Columbus, Georgia. Thompson works in the Veterans Administration office in Lafayette. The My Lai massacre occurred in 1968.

Why do we not call
Death of trees[1]
Extinction of species - holocausts?

Life with our faithful, loving mate
Is sight with two eyes
Breath through both lungs

Our whole cosmos
Is one manifestation
Of God's life-giving Love

Fullness of life expands
When we profess
Our love affair with Nature

1-The North American chestnut tree once covered the United States. An American chestnut tree is known to have survived in Bel Aire, Michigan, near Lake Bel Aire and Travis City. The only tropical rain forest remaining in the United States has been reduced to 25,000 acres and can be found on the "big island" of Hawaii. A geothermal company from Wyoming has designs upon drilling holes in the delicate ecosystem to obtain energy for the tourist industry of the islands.

We are striving to
"Bring God to others"
Where S/He is there already

Life blossoms when
We discover our deep
Intimacy with Nature

Earth, air, fire, water
Sacred sources of life
From our compassionate God

We can be blessed betwixt
Our beloved and stars
Hosting a bright moon

We bless gifts in life
Mindful of God's making them
Sacred before us

We have but one Earth
Choosing another[1]
Harms future generations

Our Universe
Answers all questions
We fail to be still and listen

So precious few purple martins
Returned this year
Silent Spring is here[2]

We know not
Our number of heartbeats
Give thanks to All while there is still time

1-Plans for life in space or in ocean depths are reminiscent of early 20th century time capsules in which life was described: "Cities of the future will have expressways where car drivers will set their speed at 100 or 150 miles per hour. The shadow of one urban sky scraper will not fall upon another building as the cities will be filled with trees and park space." (From a World's Fair in the 1920's)

2-Although *Silent Spring* by Rachel Carson in 1963 reduced the production of DDT, it remains in soil sediments and is used in nations that have not banned it. The Worldwatch Institute estimates that 6,600 out of 9,600 species of birds are having difficulty surviving.

Our sacred Earth
In some areas
Is now on a respirator

Some who have strived to serve
Find it hard
To be loved in return

A priest according to
The order of Jesus
Is Compassion lived

Fear not old age
Since life in the Spirit
Like wine is best later

We are not "lost"
If perceiving life
Drawing closer to You daily

We need more than
Degrees or computers
To touch what is going on

"Go kill the fatted calf"[1]
Does not tell us
We need meat to celebrate

Each sacred moment
Sun spirit and Earth matter
Give birth to new life

Poetry is written for
Projecting pure Truth
Rather than profits

Millions bereft of employment
Need not be
Without deep Compassion

1-In St. Luke's Gospel (chapter 15) a Forgiving Father calls for a banquet upon return of his son. Why is the Jewish mother not part of this drama?

No music or percussion
Compare to woodpeckers
With morningsong

To have deep faith
Is to be held
At the nape of our neck by Your Love

We are the first generation
Forced to co-exist
With extinction

Humble and wise people
Know that questions
Are more important than answers

Ask not - "What am I to do?"
Rather - "Who am I invited
To be?"

Full personhood depends
More upon process in our lives
Than profits[1]

Earth too daily asks of each one
"Do you really love or
Just use me?"

In the beginning was the Word[2]
Who gave birth
To our blessed DNA

"Life on high in Christ Jesus"[3]
Is deeply rooted
In daily Compassion

1-A parent in Kansas City, Missouri, expected his children to be earning $10,000 for each of their decades: at 30 the child must be earning $30,000; at 40, $40,000 and so on.

2-St. John's Gospel, Chapter 1

3-Philippians 3:14

Lacking strong defenders
In church or state
Earth is plundered

Following clear dictates
Of our conscience
Will become a full-time task

In our Earth
We see the Divine
As Mother, Father, Friend, Lover

To hold closely
To be held warmly
Daily gifts from our Loving God

Finish now
What is important for all
You may be called home quite soon

We all live
On a majestic Earth-island
Through Whom God nourishes us

Christ's Spirit
Given forth from his cross
Permeates our entire Cosmos

Like roses
Which grace our lives
We fade and return to God

Rather than lull us
Into drowsiness
Reading sparks our consciousness

Without orders
Our heart pumps
Over two million pints of blood each year

If God is with us
Who could be against us
Other than our own ego?

Loneliness too is one of our foibles
God wants to heal
Through true Love

Daily Love flowing
Through meaningful action
Satisfies our spirit

We are each one
Special gifts from the Breath
Of One who gives full Life

We pay a price
For following our conscience
Much more if we do not

We can identify
Hundreds of products
Yet do not know twelve trees

We have learned history
From the oppressed
While Earth waits for us to hear her pain

Our great ethical task
Is protecting life
For future generations

Earth calls to each one
"If you do not speak for me
How will I be heard?"

We pay a price
To reverse this throw-away world
Try living as our grandparents did

Our goal is to
Regain innocence, purity
Goodness of a child

Like children
Playing on cliffs
We do not see our relationship to Earth

In our era of falsehood
To be trusted
Is the greatest compliment

Very few have the Spirit
To ask forgiveness
For their assassins[1]

If we can forgive
The one who kills us
Why not lesser infractions?

1-Good Friday reflection - ".. .forgive them, they do not know what they are doing." (Luke 23:34)

May all our days
Be full of warm moments
Breaking bread with chosen friends

When it hurts to trash Earth
We hear voices of children
Who will follow soon

Morning silence
With the Spirit
Is nourishment for our hungry hearts

Each year we will devour
Seven hundred pounds
Of paper per person[1]

Our moon glows
By gift of sunlight
So we gleam through nearness to You

1-Research done by the Dogwood Alliance, Memphis, Tennessee. Japan is approaching the rate of paper consumption now evident in the United States.

Home is a locus of Love
Zone of silence to pray
Studio for art

To each one open to Life
God's Spirit given forth
From the cross is ours

Our Easter happens
Each day we rise
To greater sensitivity

No fire is like
Sun burning four million tons
Each second to give life[1]

Each step, every breath
Pure stringless gifts
From the One Source of all good things

1-Actual "self-consumption" in burning each moment.

Does the human or non-human world
Manifest more faith
To our God? [1]

We feel free
When believing more in ourselves
Than what others might think

Our greatest surprise
In a bureaucracy
Is being treated kindly

Are we "secure"
Seated in paper boats
Floating on seas of red ink? [2]

1-*Time* (August 11, 1997) in an article on vanishing stocks of fish, states: "It's humans, not sharks, who are Nature's most fearsome predators." (p.59)

2-The USA national debt is over $5 trillion with interest on this burden increasing at $13,000 per second.

Reflecting upon a flame
Brings us to belief
In resurrection

In our age of greed
Pure water and sanitation
Are luxuries

When reasoning is dormant
Good haiku breaks through sleep
To touch our hearts

We clear-cut Earth's forests
To build temples
Too small for God

In our brief visit to this Earth
Draw each breath
Through friendship with the One[1]

It is not easy
To answer any summons
From our Universe

1-Biblical Hebrews thought there was no name adequate for speaking of God.

If we follow sincere
Wise guiding lights
"Dis-aster" will be avoided[1]

For those in tune
With deep lyrics of Nature
It is always Earth Day

This brief visit to Earth
Is our childhood
Of eternal life with God

When we say truthfully
"I do not fear our old friend - death"
We are free[2]

1-Dis-aster means absence of a star or when a star is against someone.

2-April 29, 1998 was the beginning of another Camp Bluebird picnic in a Louisiana state park. Cancer survivors from the Lafayette area spend several days enjoying the gift of life, Nature and each other as their years, months, days dwindle down to a precious few. Together with the opening prayer, I read a new report from the Physicians for Social Responsibility in which the doctors concluded most of the cancer in our midst is due to environmental causes, not genetics.

T.S. cautioned
Our show might end
Not with a blast but one weak whimper[1]

Suspend all thought
Focus on Spirit and breath
Enter into deep prayer

Energy with blessings from our Sun
Are not withheld
From anyone

Through the World Wide Web
Nature holds us
Each moment without recompense

At the "Water Show"[2]
Nearly one hundred firms
Selling what was once pure

1-"This is how the world ends. This is how it ends. Not with a bang but a whimper." (T.S. Eliot, ***The Hollow Men***, 1925)

2-Waterwinkel, an Amsterdam boutique sold 93 brands of water in 1995 according to *Harper's Index*.

In marketing poems
Will George D. Wall forgive me
For "selling my soul"?[1]

Our acute need now
Is a leap of faith
Which perceives kinship with Earth

Where do we turn
In our day
When water is too dirty to cleanse?

1-In the hot summer of 1965 five Maryknoll theology students did community organizing in Harlem under guidance of Fr. John Calhoun of St. Thomas the Apostle Church (118th & St. Nicholas). We lived with families in Harlem. Jim Johnson and I were received by George Wall and his extended family on 122nd & Lennox. George was drafted into the British navy as a young man from Antigua, then a territory under the Queen of England. He had been to every nation with a coast, apart from a few Scandinavian countries. Breakfast with George was a travelogue. After he suffered a stroke, I asked him one day as I gave him a bath if I could sell some of his poetry written in French, Latin and English. This would help pay some medical bills. George became angry with me and snapped: "Those poems are from my innermost being and I do not sell my soul!"

Creation too says:
"This is my body"
Over billions of years now[1]

To live in the
Now and Here is to be
No-Where near anxiety

1- See *Prayer of the Universe* by Teilhard de Chardin and *Spirit of Fire* by Ursula King. She quotes him:

> "The best success I can dream for my life:
> to have spread a new vision of the world."

POSTSCRIPT

The objective of clear haiku
Just to be brief, strive to be bright
Be gone

Good haiku is
Our paramount manner
Of clear communication

Eighteeth and nineteenth century Japanese poets wrote in praise of Nature, even insects that appear unattractive to us.

Reflected
In the eye of the dragon-fly
The distant hills
- *Issa*

The three best-known haiku poets were spiritual beings because of their deep sensitivity towards Earth and Nature.

*BASHO (1644-1694) was a religious man, a poet who found God in Nature. Basho is considered the master of haiku verse and originator of this pithy style. As explained previously, in Japanese, the syllables must be 5 - 7 - 5 in three lines.

*BUSON (1715-1783) was an artist who dealt with existing things in their concrete immediacy - the here and now.

*ISSA (1763 - 1827) was a humanist, concerned with man (sic), birds and beasts in their struggle for survival. Taken from ***Silent Flowers***, Introduction, edited by Dorothy Price, Hallmark Cards, 1967).

Note: All poems without attribute are by the author.

In writing ***Tersely Yours***, volumes I, II and III, I sought pardon of the haiku masters for altering their poetry from praise of Nature to defense of the natural beauty which is vanishing fast. They had a far greater share of the majestic gifts in Nature than we who live in the closing days of the 20th century. Today we face a ruthless "moonscaping" of Earth in the name of jobs. Even when employment is toxic to workers, the pursuit of profit and endless development continue.

These three small volumes were written out of concern for future generations who should not be deprived of simple encounters with trees, plants and animals.

A Cajun is a descendant of those expelled from Europe, Nova Scotia, and eventually settled in Louisiana. Apart from the extremely brief explanation, a Cajun has been described as "someone who will survive, no matter what."

Cajuns cling to traditional religious beliefs. Along with their church membership, time with Nature is essential for the spiritual well-being of the Cajun culture.

"Boudreaux" jokes are inescapable. At the funeral home, Mrs. Boudreaux was asked what she wanted in her husband's obituary. When told by the undertaker the cost would be about one dollar per word, she suggested, " 'Boudreaux dead,' that's enough." The friendly mortician suggested she go to one side of the home, reflect, pray for a moment and come up with something more encouraging than 'Boudreaux dead.' She returned after a time of reflection and said, "Make it five words - 'Boudreaux dead - boat for sale.' "

Rugged Cajun folk know that Nature is our ultimate teacher.

Cajuns fishing are cautioning
"Mother Nature biting back.
hhhaaarrrd too."

- *National Geographic*,
August 1977, p.22

Love of Nature is the bond between haiku poets and Cajuns.

These volumes of haiku poems were written on behalf of "Dead Giants." (This is a term of Cajun writer Greg Giurard for the 2000-year-old cypress trees which have been clear-cut.)

Neither native dwellers nor visitors will have the experience of boating in the midst of such trees.

Over 400 species of birds have been sighted in Louisiana. They are members of a global family of some 9,600 species of birds observed by Lester Brown and members of the Worldwatch Institute. In a recent report, the Institute considers that "6,600 are in decline. Of these, the populations of some 1000 species have dropped to the point where they are threatened with extinction." (*State of the World*, 1995, p.4)

The Louisiana alligators have no threats other than hunters who seek their skins for purses, belts and then sell the meat to restaurants.

Fearless alligators
Laze about
For sixty-five million years now

In addition to the hunters, alligators are threatened by chemicals, fertilizers and offal from over thirty states to the north introduced into Louisiana by way of the Mississippi.

Through a telescopic lens one can study the alligators at ease, breathing infrequently and "eating the Sun," along with anything that moves within a few feet of those powerful jaws. All living beings are affected by the chemical invasion of our environments. Alligators in Florida have been found without penises, or other deformities.

Gators quiz "big-brained
Two-legged ones"[1]
What think you of the next million years?

1-Novelist Kurt Vonnegut's description of the human.

For the Atchafalaya and Cajuns

Greg Giurard is a modern Cajun writer who both defends and glorifies Nature in his books. ***The Land of Dead Giants*** (cypress trees gone forever) and ***Atchafalaya Autumn*** portray the one-time endowment of Nature, now under threat from logging, farming and development.

Cajun Families of the Atchafalaya is a series of interviews with Cajuns who have witnessed the degradation of bayou territory into which they were born. There are photos of large fish, 12-foot long alligators and touching dialogues with Cajuns who are bonded to the territory.

There is a beautiful photo of Cezaire Bonin, carrying Yolande, his paralyzed wife, on his back to a boat where she is strapped in for a fishing trip.

Though not compressed into haiku form, *Ballad of the Atchafalaya* by Errol Verret captures the concise skills of Basho and his cohorts:

I think of the future
I think of the past
And I wonder
What will become of this place
I hope to see a future
Where the young will comprehend and respect
What the eyes of the old people
Have seen in the past

- From***Cajun Families of the Atchafalaya***

My eyes, having seen all,
Come back to
The white chrysanthemums

- *Issho*

All around
That meets the eye
Is cool and fresh

- *Basho*

Basho and Cajuns Joined by Yogi Berra

Yogi Berra was a great catcher for the New York Yankees, known for his sense of humor along with baseball prowess. Berra offered this advice: "If you come to a fork in the road - take it."

Humankind reached that ecological juncture in history long ago. And we have taken both roads.

One is marked - *Rue De Harmony*

The other is named, but without visible warnings

- *Rue De Chaos.*

Dr. Gerald Barney directed the *Global Report to the President*. He spoke to The Foundation For a Global Community (California) in the summer of 1996. Dr. Barney does not believe we have made enough improvements in our relationship with Earth and cautions:

"Considering everything, I conclude these trends (our wanton destruction of life systems) CANNOT CONTINUE FOR MORE THAN ANOTHER GENERATION - AT MOST A HUNDRED YEARS. (emphasis is mine). Something needs to be done in that time, and I see no reason why we can't do a whole lot different and better than we are now doing. (*The Millenium: Threshold for Change, **Timeline***, July/August 1996)

Giving ourselves no more than another generation, or one hundred years, does not make Dr. Barney appear as a dismal prognosticator of the end of history. His comments are in sync with the thinking of Native Americans who have never broken their bonds with a sacred Earth.

We cannot go on
InTOXICating Earth
And have hope for our future

Barney does not appear as an alarmist when his words are coupled with scholars such as E. O. Wilson, a Harvard biologist and author of the Pulitzer Prize Winning book, ***The Diversity of Life***.

Wilson and Barney point out a major blockage to change.

"Exceptionalism" is a false belief that the God of my faith will intervene and protect us from environmental chaos. The Divine will not let us travel *Rue De Chaos.*

However, fourth grade students are fully aware of the fact we have poisoned all major rivers of the world and suitable drinking water is increasingly difficult to obtain. Those who live on both sides of the Rio Grande River know that 800 toxins have made it impossible for drinking in Mexico or the United States.

Milestones on Rue De Harmony

Gradual awakening of the churches is a hopeful sign in this time when Earth begs for greater literacy and awareness. There are over 400,000 houses of worship in the United States. If informed, they could be a very powerful constituency in the effort to bring about environmental reformation.

If only the churches awake in time.

In the 1990's, an ecumenical effort by the major denominations raised $4.3 million to publish ***Renewing the Earth***, an educational kit to bring environmental awareness to a higher level.

This ecumenical-environmental endeavor brought about strong criticism from *The Wall Street Journal*. This paper perceived the churches could form a large block of resistance to unlimited financial growth if this came at the expense of Nature. Life for CEO's could become quite complicated. As corporate heads, they will seek unlimited growth while spiritual leaders advocate respect for the gifts of Earth over financial gain.

By educating people of faith that the United States has the largest Gross National Product (GNP) in the world, that we are the greatest consumer of energy, resources and, consequently, that we generate more wastes than any other country, there might be an inclination towards restraint over unlimited growth.

The Environmental Protection Agency (EPA) has established and enforced strick regulations on handling our own wastes. In doing so, a "global dumping" system has evolved in which the poorest nations of the world are victimized. Conscience might lead church leaders to denounce cities such as Philadelphia for dumping a barge full of toxic ashes on the beaches of Haiti in 1986. The ashes were still there in the summer of 1998.

Is God "Powerless"?

The late Penny Lernoux was a prophetic and prolific writer who died on October 8th, 1989 at 49 years of age. This young victim of cancer once said to Benedictine Sister Joan Chittister, "God is powerless."

If love from God is going to reach a child, such a gift will be received through loving parents, family and indeed the whole village.

Added to this awareness, we admit God did not prevent 8000 wars in 10,000 years of history. The fiction of "exceptionalism," with regard to care of Earth, will lead us to awareness of the fact that we all cooperate with God to protect the Earth which gives us life.

To care for the Earth
Is to share with God
In the act of creation

- *Prayer of the Columban Fathers*

The Greening of Three States

Bill McKibben, author of *The End of Nature*, was asked by David Brower to write a book with stories about how there has been a dramatic turnabout and recovery of Nature.

In his latest book, ***Hope, Human and Wild***, McKibben uses New Hampshire as an example of an area where forests were clear-cut in the 19th century. "Despite increases in population, 90 percent of New Hampshire is covered by forests. Vermont has gone from 35 percent woods in 1850 to 80 percent today, and even Massachusetts has seen its woodlands rebound to the point where they cover nearly two-thirds of the commonwealth." (*Timeline*, May/June 1998, book review by Mac Lawrence)

There is not one scientist who would dispute the fact carbon dioxide has been building up continually since the 1800's. At the same time, there is an inverse proportion as trees which absorb carbon dioxide are being removed from the face of Earth.

Clearcutting trees which faithfully generate oxygen and take in carbon dioxide will have a negative impact upon all who dwell upon Spaceship Earth.

Before Russia welcomed the free market system, the city of Kiev held to a policy of not selling cars unless a sufficient number of trees were present to take in the carbon dioxide from vehicles. (Recall that 22 1bs. of carbon dioxide are generated by each gallon of gasoline).

On a global scale, it is presumed that Japan has far more factories than forests to cope with the carbon dioxide. The oxygen generated by Amazon rain forests cannot continue to make up for the loss of oxygen worldwide. This simple assumption applies to all nations.

The "greening" of three small states will not suffice in our daily quest for oxygen. A land mass the size of Australia would have to be covered with trees to maintain a balance of producing oxygen while absorbing the carbon dioxide we generate.

The present imbalance contributes to global warming as six billion tons of carbon tons of carbon dioxide are forced into the limited space which constitutes our atmosphere.

A man from San Antonio who grew up in Houston recalls his childhood when rain fell every day around 4 o'clock. As the city sprawled out, removing trees and swallowing up farms by paving over the land, those rains no longer visited the city. Foul air from Pasadena and other refinery cities to the east then blanketed Houston.

As trees disappear in Texas, it is known to those who study environmental events that Texas generates more carbon dioxide than any other state in the union. Only six nations in the world account for more carbon dioxide than Texas.

The world
Is after all the butterfly
However it may be
- *Soin*

Anyone who walks the Appalachian Trail, or takes a stroll in the countryside, is already aware of streams without fish or any marine life. There are occasional signs warning of polluted water. However, birds and other creatures in the woods do not understand the signs. They suffer consequences we take measures to avoid.

A brief passage from just one newsletter prepared by researchers with *Rachel's Hazardous Waste News*, (now titled *Rachel's Health & Environment Weekly*) is sufficient to determine how extensive our chemical inundation of Earth has become.

The report was prepared by two scientists from the Oak Ridge National Laboratory (Tennessee) and is not a study done by a "deep ecology" group. Curtis Travis and Sheri Hester have given us an objective prognosis of the planet:

"(T)hey confirmed what many people already knew: THE ENTIRE SURFACE IS POLLUTED." (emphasis is mine)

The moon in the water
Turned a somersault
And floated away
- *Ryota*

By lacing our beautiful land and water with chemicals we have made life for future generations less healthy.

Our struggle now is for preservation of the air. Our visit to this planet cannot continue for more than two minutes without fresh air.

The American Lung Cancer Association has as its logo:

If You Can't Breathe, Not Much Else Matters

Passage of legislation to protect our air has evolved into a complicated commercialized game of "pollution trade-offs" between cities that are in compliance with some aspects of the law and others that are not. It's all too complicated for ordinary citizens whose lungs are hurt by the bureaucracy.

Grasshopper -
Do not trample to pieces
The pearls of bright dew
- *Issa*

Can We Learn From Frogs and Chickadees?

May of 1998 was the driest month on record in south Louisiana. The dry spell gripped the state until late June when farmers hopes were lifted with several days of rain. Frogs in the bayous and urban areas rejoiced in the long-awaited precipitation.

Audubon (May-June 1997) carried a lengthy article on frogs, replete with beautiful photos of exotic amphibians.

In a scientific, non-poetic form of speech, a scientist said:

"The frogs seem to be telling us something. We'd better find out what it is, and soon." The same herpetologist states that nearly one-third of frogs and toads in the United States are imperilled.

Photos of frogs born with deformities are found in daily newspapers. Chemical pollution, harm from ultra-violet rays of the Sun, and loss of habitat are major causes for the decline in frogs.

Since they are fading fast
Don't miss your chance
To pet a neighborhood frog
- *Tersely Yours, II, p. 29.*

Or kiss the little creature if you like. No warts will come to disfigure us.

The sound of tears
Hissing, quenching
The banked charcoal
- *Basho*

The chemical invasion of our environment has become so thorough that even breast milk, the purest form of human nutrition, has been rendered less wholesome. (See footnote #2 on page 43.)

Children, and those yet to be born, are the most vulnerable.

CHILDREN FROM THE AGES OF 0 - 4 YEARS
18% increase in leukemia
32% increase in kidney and renal pelvic cancer
37% increase in soft tissue cancers
53% increase in brain and nervous system cancers

TEENAGERS BETWEEN THE AGES OF 15 - 19 YEARS
29% increase in thyroid problems
128% increase in Non-Hidgkin Lymphoma (Hodgkin)
78% increase in ovarian cancer
65% increase in testis cancer
39% increase in bone and joint cancers

- Center For Health, Environment
and Justice, Falls Church, Virginia.

Can We Form A New Brain For Survival?

In the 1990's neurobiologists discovered the Black-Capped Chickadee formed new brain cells during seed-hiding time.
- *The New York Times*, November 15th, 1994.

Scientists are far from determining if such possibilities apply to species other than birds. Dr. Fernando Nottebohm explained, "Humans can sprout new synaptic connections throughout life but must largely make do with the neurons received at birth." Another neurobiologist, Dr. Eric Kandel, responds with skepticism toward the possibility of forming new parts in the brain, "I've told Fernando that what he is doing is wonderful poetry."

Although the suggestion of forming new parts in our brain may appear as poetic fiction, the cancer statistics, upheavals of Nature and unprecedented rate of animal extinction in our era prompt us to pursue a completely new way of thinking.

Is not a "sea change" in consciousness tantamount to a "new brain"?

Railing against nuclear weaponry is an example of the new consciousness no longer limited to utopian pacifists. After 45 years in the United States Navy, Admiral Noel Gaylor testified he would not even allow a nuclear weapon under his command, so horrible are they in their destructive capacity. (***Tersely Yours, Vol. II***, p. 44.)

The corporate world in the form of "Big Tobacco" and other obtuse CEO's still adhere to a state of denial and continue ruination of waterways together with the health of communities.

General Electric is under pressure to spend billions for the cleanup of the majestic Hudson River, flowing into New York City. John F. Welch, Jr., GE's chairman, responded to public pressure by stating, "We simply do not believe there are any adverse health effects from PCB's."

This position from a GE official is not congruent with the Environmental Protection Agency (EPA) which declared the Hudson a Superfund Site and warned citizens of the danger in eating fish whose flesh contains PCB's. (*The Citizen's Register*, White Plains, New York - 14 June 1998)

In line with chickadees
We are asked to form new brains
For our future

Economics continues to dominate our consciousness. The word for "profit" in Hebrew is "to cut or make an incision." The quest for profit and economic growth has cut deeply into the health of Earth which gives life and nourishment to us.

With the fall of the Berlin Wall, there is a mad rush to join the "free market" system. Kirkpatrick Sale is an iconoclastic voice in a world which bows to Harvard economists. Sale observes, "If it had been the design of human history to bring the world to the edge of ruin, there could be no better mechanism than the free market economy."

Coming generations
Might exude care of Earth
Over all pursuits

Consciousness will help us perceive that industrial plundering of the planet has brought about a "Toxic Time Bomb" that will be an ongoing attack on all creatures, human and nonhuman, yet to be born. The "new brain" will evolve into an awareness for which Thomas Berry longs. It is the "Ecozoic Age." This is the geological period flowing from the Cenozoic. As we blindly march on destroying the Cenozoic, with the inspiration of a loving Creator this yet-to-be defined age will break forth like a butterfly from its shell. If we are to survive, this period will be the moment in time when special care of Earth becomes the sacred vocation of everyone.

Scientific documentation for all of the above poems and warnings in Postscript comments can be found in studying the books of two female prophets of the 20th century. Rachel Carson's ***Silent Spring***, still remains the most important book of the past fifty years. ***Our Stolen Future*** by Theo Coburn and her research associates is a sequel to Carson's book. It was ***Silent Spring*** that changed the life of Caesar Chavez, and will bring about a change in the consciousness of anyone who dares to read the book carefully.

This book exposed DDT and brought about the demise of this chemical before it brought about the end for Bald Eagles.

What DDT was to the 1960's, dioxin is to the 1990's. Lois Gibbs, yet another heroic female of the 20th century, exposed the damage wrought by dioxin in Love Canal. DDT still lurks in the sediment of waters from which we draw fish for daily consumption. Dioxin is in our food and air, but not yet the subject of conversation.

Our true
Fullness of salvation includes
Body and soul at all times

Reprint of:
RACHEL'S HAZARDOUS WASTE NEWS #234
Providing news and resources for environmental justice
— May 22, 1991

Chemical Regulation-Part I:
PUSH COMES TO SHOVE

Two researchers from Oak Ridge National Laboratory (ORNL), Curtis Travis and Sheri Hester, have just published a new study of chemical contamination of planet Earth and have confirmed what many people already knew: **THE ENTIRE SURFACE IS POLLUTED**. What separates Travis and Hester from other U.S. Government researchers before them is their stated belief that all this pollution is taking its toll on human health: "We maintain that ambient [normal, everyday] levels of pollution have risen to the point where human health is being affected on a global scale." Furthermore, they conclude that planet-wide contamination seems certain to increase because U.S. Environmental Protection Agency (EPA) does not even try to prevent the spread of low levels of chemicals through air, water, and soil. EPA's regulatory programs have other goals.

EPA's regulatory programs are aimed at protecting the most-exposed individual near any given facility. Whether it's mercury released from a municipal solid waste incinerator or radioactivity released into water from a low-level radioactive waste dump, EPA's regulations say, "Our goal is to protect the individual who may be getting the biggest exposure." EPA, therefore, picks a spot where they believe the greatest exposure will occur, then EPA establishes the concentration (in parts per million) that they believe the individual can "safely" receive during a lifetime of exposure. They define "safe" as "an exposure that will kill no more than one in every million individuals so exposed." EPA then figures out, as best they can, these goals (and assumptions about dilution), EPA then issues a permit for a particular polluter to release a certain amount of mercury (or radioactivity, or other toxin) into air or water continuously. Since the allowable release is set to protect the maximally-exposed individual, EPA assumes all is well, never considering the buildup from many "safe" releases.

One could raise doubts about many aspects of this approach to pollution control, but the ORNL researchers highlighted only one key problem: continuous releases of mercury (or radioactivity, or other toxin), although they may protect the most-exposed individual, do nevertheless allow toxic materials to enter the environment continuously. Toxics released from thousands, or perhaps millions, of different sources add up. Additional "adding up" occurs in the food chain. A low concentration of mercury in water turns into a slightly higher concentration in plants living in that water, an even higher concentration in animals eating those plants, and so on up the food chain. You may start off with a small dose in air or water, but large predators at the top of the food chain (big fish, big birds; wolves, humans, bears, etc.) get a large dose.

Once they are released into the environment, chemicals seek out the environmental medium (air, water, soil, or living things) in which they are most soluble. Trichloroethylene (TCE) and benzene are most soluble in air, so they tend to be found in air. DDT and PCBs are most soluble in the fatty tissues of living things, so they tend to move into the food chain and concentrate in living things.

Transport through the atmosphere is the main way that chemicals spread around the globe; even fat-soluble chemicals initially move via the atmosphere, then they enter food chains and concentrate in animals (including humans). So most pollutants travel via the atmosphere, but food is the main source of pollutants for humans.

Travis and Hester focus on PCBs, dioxins, benzene, mercury, and lead, showing how "ambient" (normal, everyday background)

they can, how much dilution will occur from the point of release to the place where the most-exposed individual resides. Based on levels of these contaminants are high enough to make people sick. They make the point—worth emphasizing—that they chose these chemicals because data exists for these chemicals. For the vast majority of chemicals we dump into the air and water routinely via incinerators, landfills, and intentional releases from factory pipes and stacks, no data exists on how much is dumped, where it goes, or what effects it may be having. EPA has spent 20 years not gathering the relevant data.

PCBs. Although Congress banned PCBs in 1976 and EPA banned them in 1977, an estimated 900 tons of PCBs cycle through the U.S. atmosphere each year. Somewhere between 60% and 90% of the PCBs entering the Great Lakes come from the atmosphere, according to Travis and Hester. The average PCB concentration in breast milk in the U.S. is 89 micrograms per kilogram. They calculate that the background level of PCBs in the U.S. food supply creates a cancer risk of 110 per million (using EPA's method for calculating cancer risks). That is to say, among every group of one-million U.S. citizens [and there are 245 such groups in our population of 245 million people], 110 individuals can be expected to get cancer from normal, background PCB exposures.

Dioxins. Background dioxin levels in the American people are lower than PCB levels, but dioxins are more potent carcinogens than PCBs. The "background" cancer risk from dioxins, according to Travis and Hester, is 210 per million.

Benzene. The background cancer risk from routine exposure to benzinein the U.S. in 100 per million (or one in 10,000).

Mercury. Travis and Hester do not calculate a cancer risk for mercury. However, they make the important point that mercury released by coal combustion, by the chlor-alkali industry (which produces chlorine and caustic soda), and by municipal waste incinerators has introduced mercury into enormous areas far distant from the places where the mercury was released. In remote lakes in Michigan, 15% of the fish contain mercury concentrations in excess of that state's health advisory of 0.5 parts per million (ppm). Approximately 30% of Wisconsin's lakes and 50% of Florida's lakes contain fish with mercury levels that exceed state health standards. Mercury seems to becoming a global problem, not limited to areas near point-sources.

Lead. Travis and Hester report that lead is affecting between 3 and 4 million U.S. children adversely (chiefly impaired cognitive development—stunted mental growth) because of "our mismanagement and heavy use of this toxic material." An additional 400,000 fetuses in the U.S. are probably harmed by lead each year before they are born, Travis and Hester report.

Travis and Hester calculated the background cancer risk from 11 chemicals, using data from the U.S. Department of Agriculture (which samples the U.S. food supply for chemicals occasionally) and using EPA's method of calculating cancer risks. They conclude that these 11 chemicals create a background cancer risk of 1000 in a million, or one in a thousand. And of course this does not consider consequences besides cancer. It omits consideration of respiratory problems, reproductive and developmental illnesses, nervous system disorders, damage to the immune system, the increasing occurrence of multiple chemical sensitivity (see RHWN *#16S, #220)* and much more.

Travis and Hester's cancer analysis is based on a tiny part of the full picture. They say, 'The true extent of human exposure to environmental pollution has never been quantified. For example, the [EPA's] human adipose [fatty] tissue survey has identified only a very small fraction of the chemical mass found in human adipose tissue." In other words, no data exist for the vast majority of chemical exposures that are occurring routinely. EPA has studiously avoided gathering the data.

As for *solving* this problem, don't look to EPA. Travis and Hester say, "The only way to diminish global cycling of contaminants is to decrease production of' pollutants or to destroy pollutants before they are released into the environment.... At present, the most commonly used method to destroy pollutants is incineration. However, emissions from incinerator stacks tend to release pollutants directly into the atmosphere." EPA has placed all its eggs in the incineration basket and is aggressively trying to force all states to site incinerators (see RHWN *#142)—a* strategy guaranteed to make the problem of global contamination worse. As for the suggestion to "decrease production of pollutants," this would require governmental intrusion into the manufacturing place, compelling factory owners to stop using certain chemicals, or to use less of them. Travis and Hester argue this is the only way to prevent global contamination, with its attendant human health damage. Thus is seems to come down to this: the health of humans in general vs. the right of American manufacturers to call the shots inside their own factories. Push really *has* come to shove. Fireworks ahead.

Get: Curtis C. Travis and Sheri T; Hester, "Global Chemical Pollution," *Environmental Science and Technology Vol.25,* No.5 (May, 1991), pgs. 814-819.

Rachel's Hazardous Waste News (ISSN 10654623) is published weekly by Environmental Research Foundation (ERF), P.O. Box 5036, Annapolis, MD 21403-7036; Telephone: (410) 263-1584; Fax: (410) 263-8944; E-mail: erf@rachel.clark.net. Editor: Peter Montague, Ph.D. Please contact us for current subscription rates or to receive a free, four-week trial subscription.

About the Author

Vic Hummert is from Breese, Illinois. This is a town in southern Illinois that does not have an industrial smoke stack, nor an expressway. And there still has not been a murder since its founding in 1856.

From this tranquil, rural environment he went to Hong Kong, the most densely populated region of the world for a ten year experience as a missioner- social worker-factory employee to work an eight-hour day in a toy company for $2.30.

Vic Hummert

Since 1989 he has been in the two most "environmentally" disadvantaged states of the union - Texas and Louisiana. During these years there has been a continual effort to be a voice in a wilderness known as "cancer corridor." The reluctance to hear long explanations about environmental degradation has evolved into the practice of expressing our harmony - or lack of - with Earth in three lines.

A large bookstore chain asked that Vic establish his own firm and name himself as president so they might place ***Tersely Yours*** on its shelves for sale. Earth Literacy is a company that will never make the business pages of the Lafayette daily paper. He resides with his wife Roselyn in this city of 108,000 people.